Romantic Rhapsody

Quotes from the Heart

compiled by
Julie Otlewis

0 43422 69552 2

Cover Design by Roy Honegger

Published by Great Quotations Publishing Co.,
Glendale Heights, IL

Library of Congress Catalog Card Number: 95-81335

ISBN 1-56245-239-8

Printed in Hong Kong

When marrying,
one should ask oneself this question:
Do you believe that you will be able to converse
well with this woman into your old age?

— Nietzsche

Union of hearts,
not hands, does a marriage make,
And sympathy of mind keeps love awake.

— Aaron Hill

*The courage to share your feelings is
critical to sustaining a love relationship.*

— Harold H. Bloomfield

To love is to receive a glimpse of heaven.

— Karen Sunde

A house is made of walls and beams;
a home is built with love and dreams.

There is only one kind of love,
but there are a thousand different versions.

— La Rochefoucauld

Love is as strict as acting.
If you want to love somebody,
stand there and do it. If you don't, don't.
There are no other choices.

— Tyne Daly

Hearts are not had
as a gift but hearts
are earned . . .

— William Butler Yeats

Love is a power too strong to be overcome
by anything but flight.

— Cervantes

If you have love in your life, you can
make up for a great many things you lack.
If you don't have it, no matter what else there is,
it's not enough.

Love many things, for therein lies the true strength,
and whosoever loves much performs much,
and can accomplish much, and what is done
in love is done well.

— Vincent van Gogh

Until I truly loved,
I was alone.

— Caroline Sheridan Nordon

Friend: one who knows
all about you and loves you just the same.

— Elbert Hubbard

Love doesn't make the world go 'round,
but it makes the ride worthwhile.

Of all the music that reached farthest into heaven,
it is the beating of a loving heart.

— Henry Ward Beecher

*Love is often a
fruit of marriage.*

— Moliere

*Marriage is popular because it combines
the maximum of temptation with the
maximum of opportunity.*

— Bernard Shaw

*You have to work constantly at rejuvenating
a relationship. You can't just count on its
being O.K.; or it will tend toward a
hollow commitment, devoid of passion
and intimacy. People need to put the kind of energy
into it that they put into their children or career.*

— Dr. Robert Sternberg

*There is only one way to happiness
and that is to cease worrying about things
which are beyond our control.*

— Epictetus

Love must be learned, and learned again
and again; there is no end to it.

— Katherine Ann Porter

You can give without loving,
but you can't love without giving.

The giving of love is an education in itself.

— Eleanor Roosevelt

A lady of forty-seven who has been married twenty-seven years and has six children knows what love really is and once described it for me like this. Love is what you've been through with somebody."

— James Thurber

*If the husband and wife can possibly afford it,
they should definitely have separate bathrooms
for the sake of their marriage.*

— Doris Day

Too much honesty did never man harm.

— John Clarke

Any time that is not spent on love is wasted.

— Torquato Tasso

We find rest in those
we love, and we provide
a resting place in ourselves for
those who love us.

— Saint Bernard of Clairvaux

Love is the only weapon we need.

— Rev. H. R. L. Sheppard

*True love doesn't have a happy ending;
true love doesn't have an ending.*

*Never idealize others. They will never live up to
your expectations. Don't overanalyze
your relationships. Stop playing games,
a growing relationship can only be
nurtured by genuineness.*

— Leo Buscaglia

The best and most beautiful things in the world
cannot be seen, nor touched . . .
but are felt in the heart.

— Helen Keller

Two persons must believe in each other,
and feel that it can be done and must be done;
in that way they are enormously strong.
They must keep up each other's courage.

— Vincent van Gogh

In marriage do thou be wise;
prefer the person before money;
virtue before beauty; the mind before the body.

— William Penn

Love is but the discovery of ourselves in others,
and the delight in the recognition.

— Alexander Smith

Married couples who claim they've never had an argument in forty years either have poor memories or a very dull life to recall.

Love is, above all
the gift of oneself.

— Jean Anouilh

*For love is but the heart's immortal thirst
to be completely known and all forgiven.*

Henry van Dyke

*Love is a canvas furnished by nature
and embroidered by imagination.*

— Voltaire

No love, no friendship
can cross the path of our destiny without leaving
some mark on it forever.

— Francois Mauriac

You shouldn't go into a relationship expecting that he or she will change. If you pick your mate wisely, you will both make adjustments, but it's unfair to expect your future mate to make basic changes. Put yourself in his or her shoes. Would you want to be overhauled or would you expect your mate to love you as you are?

— Dr. Zev Wanderer and Erika Fabian

Ay, marriage is the lifelong miracle,
the self-begetting wonder, daily fresh.

— Charles Kingsley

Marriage is the result of the longing for the deep, deep peace of the double bed after the hurly-burly of the chaise-lounge.

— Mrs Pat Campbell

Marriage today must...be concerned not with the inviable commitment of constancy and unending passion, but with patterns of liberty and discovery.

— Carolyn Heilbrun

The supreme happiness of life is the conviction that we are loved.

— Victor Hugo

*It is very important to make sure the
person you're marrying is likeminded.
It's crucial for a couple to have shared goals
and values. The more you have in common
the less you have to argue about.*

— Barbara Friedman

*Where love is concerned,
too much is not even enough.*

— Pierre-Augustin de Beaumarchais

*Success in marriage is more than finding
the right person. It's also a matter
of being the right person.*

The most brilliant achievement was to be able to persuade my wife to marry me.

— Winston Churchill

*The advantage of being married to
an archaeologist is that the older one grows
the more interested he becomes.*

— Agatha Christie

To love is to choose.

— Joseph Roux

Marriage: that I call the will of two to create the one who is more than those who created it.

— Friedrich Nietzsche

Nothing makes a marriage rust like distrust.

*Marriage must exemplify friendship's
highest ideal, or else it will be a failure.*

— Margaret E. Sangster

But there's nothing half so sweet in life
As love's young dream.

— Clement C. Moore

*It is better to know as little as possible
of the defects of the person with whom
you are to pass your life.*

— Jane Austin

*We always believe our first love is our last,
and our last love our first.*

— George Whyte-Melville

Marriage is a wonderful invention;
but then so is a bicycle repair kit.

— Billy Connolly

Love is all we have, the only way that each can help the other.

— Euripides

Not caged, my bird, my sweet bird,
But nested - nested.

— Habberton Lulham

It takes patience to appreciate domestic bliss,
volatile spirits prefer unhappiness.

— George Santayana

You must not contrast too strongly the hours of courtship with the years of possession.

— Benjamin Disraeli

*A husband should tell his wife everything
that he is sure she will find out,
and before anyone else does.*

— Thomas Robert Dewar

*There is nothing nobler or more admirable
than when two people who see eye to eye
keep house as man and wife,
confounding their enemies and
delighting their friends.*

— Homer

Love:
To feel with one's whole self the existence
of another being.

— Simone Weil

*One does not find happiness in marriage,
but takes happiness into marriage.*

Love is to the moral nature exactly
what the sun is to the earth.

— Honore De Balzac

*One word frees us of all
the weight and pain of life:
That word is love.*

— Sophocles

As I am true to thee and thine,
Do thou be true to me and mine.

— Scott

Don't let your marriage go stale.
Change the bag on the Hoover of life.

— Victoria Wood

A good marriage is the key that opens the gates of happiness.

If I know what love is, it is because of you.

— Herman Hesse

*True it is that marriages be done in heaven
and performed on earth.*

— William Painter

Marriages are made in Heaven.

— Alfred Lord Tennyson

*The grand essentials of happiness are
something to do, something to love,
and something to hope for.*

Love is a feeling of beautiful want
one person can bring to your heart,
and a feeling of loneliness deep down inside
whenever you must be apart.

There is no more lovely, friendly and charming relationship, communion or company than a good marriage.

— Martin Luther

He who gives to me teaches me to give.

— Danish Proverb

Love is the strange bewilderment which overtakes one person on account of another person.

— James Thurber and E. B. White

*Love does not consist in gazing at each other
but in looking together in the same direction.*

— Antoine de Saint-Exupery

*To love someone is to be the only one to
see a miracle invisible to others.*

— Francois Mauriac

I like not only to be loved,
but to be told I am loved.

— George Eliot

Love is supreme and unconditional;
like is nice but limited.

— Duke Ellington

*It is not a lack of love, but a lack of friendship
that makes unhappy marriages.*

— Nietzsche

Oh love, as long as you can love.

— Ferdinand Freiligrath

A successful marriage is one in which you fall in love many times, always with the same person.

— McLaughlin

*Between whom there is hearty truth
there is love . . .*

— Henry David Thoreau

To love but little is in love an infallible means of being beloved.

— La Rochefoucauld

We learn only from those we love.

— Goethe

Youth's for an hour, beauty's a flower,
But love is the jewel that wins the world.

— Moira O'Neill

Grow old along with me!
The best is yet to be,
The last of life, for which the first was made.

— Matthew Arnold

The only true gift is a portion of yourself.

— Ralph Waldo Emerson

O thou who has given us so much,
mercifully grant us one thing more -
a grateful heart.

— George Herbert

*Two souls with but a single thought,
two hearts that beat as one.*

— Von Munch Bellinghausen

Give all to love;
Obey thy heart . . .

— Ralph Waldo Emerson

*The most precious possession that ever
comes to a man in this world is a woman's heart.*

— Holland

Who ever lov'd, that lov'd not at first sight?

— Christopher Marlowe

*A happy marriage has in it all the pleasures
of friendships, all the enjoyments of sense and
reason - and indeed all the sweets of life.*

— Joseph Addison

Love is a little word, make it big.

*The supreme happiness of life is the
conviction that we are loved.*

— Victor Hugo

True hearts that share one love, one life,
will always know true joy.

— Jason Blake

*There is no more lovely, friendly
and charming relationship,
communion or company than a good marriage.*

— Martin Luther

When Adam was lonely,
God created for him not ten friends,
but one wife.

*At the beginning of a marriage ask yourself
whether this woman will be interesting to talk to
from now until old age. Everything else in
marriage is transitory: most of the time
is spent in conversation.*

— Friedrich Nietzsche

*If one wants marriage to be a refuge
friendship must gradually replace love.*

— Alain

It is kindness in a person, not beauty,
that wins our love.

Only choose in marriage a woman whom you would choose as a friend if she were a man.

— Joseph Joubert

Let there be spaces in togetherness.

— Kahlil Gibran

Love is the wine of existence.

— Henry Ward Beecher

*The real value of love is the increased
general vitality it produces.*

— Paul Valery

Love is sharing a part of yourself with others.

The critical period in matrimony is breakfast time.

— A. P. Herbert

One year of joy, another of comfort,
and all the rest of content.

— John Ray

*Actually, I believe in marriage,
having done it three times.*

— Joan Collins

What's the earth
With all its art, verse, music, worth -
Compared with love found, gained, and kept?

— Robert Browning

There is no beauty so great as beauty shared.

*Seldom, or perhaps never does a marriage
develop into an individual relationship smoothly
and without crises; there is no coming
to consciousness without pain.*

— Carl Jung

*Love is always in the mood of
believing in miracles.*

— John Cowper Powys

*Of all forms of caution, caution in love
is perhaps the most fatal to true happiness.*

— Bertrand Russell

The love we have in our youth is superficial compared to the love that an old man has for his old wife.

— Wil Durant

*I believe that we should all wise up
and recognize that a marriage is a small business
and all married couples are business partners.*

— David Hopkinson

God the best maker of all marriages
Combine your hearts in one.

— Shakespeare

Marriages are made in heaven
but are lived on earth.

*What marriage needs is more open minds
and fewer open mouths.*

For I do love you . . .
as the dew loves the flowers;
as the birds love the sunshine;
as the wavelets love the breeze.

— Mark Twain

Marriage may be inspired by music, soft words, and perfume; but its security is manifest in work, consideration and respect.

The joys of marriage are the heaven on earth,
Life's paradise, great princess, the soul's quiet,
Sinews of concord, earthly immortality,
Eternity of pleasure.

— John Ford

Making marriage work is like operating a farm. You have to start all over again each morning.

Love has no other desire but to fulfill itself.
To melt and be like running brook that
sings its melody to the night.
To wake at dawn with a winged heart and
give thanks for another day of loving.

— Kahlil Gibran

*The bonds of matrimony are like
any other bond - they take a while to mature.*

Appreciate what you have before you haven't.

As your wedding ring wears,
You'll wear off your cares.

— Thomas Fuller

Grow with your husband.
Remember that he lives in an enlarging world.
Make yours the same.

— A wife in her sixties

But happy they!
The happiest of their kind!
Whom gentler stars unite, and in one fate
Their hearts, their fortunes, and their beings blend.

— Thomson

When you marry . . . make sure your lives
are different enough so that you have
something to tell each other in the evening.

— Brett Daniels

My mother said: "Marry a man with good teeth and high arches." She thought I should get that into the genetic structure of the family.

— Jill Clayburgh

How do I love thee?
Let me count the ways.
I love thee to the depth
and breadth and height
my soul can reach.

— Elizabeth Barret Browning

*If you have respect and consideration
for one another, you'll make it.*

— Mary Durso (married 58 years)

Be courteous! Why are husbands and wives more courteous to strangers than to each other?

*To keep the fire burning brightly there's one
easy rule: Keep the two logs together,
near enough to keep each other
warm and far enough apart -
about a finger's breadth - for breathing room.
Good fire, good marriage, same rule.*

— Marnie Reed Crowel

If you would be loved, love.

— Hecato

Commit yourself to a dream . . .
Nobody who tries to do something great
but fails is a total failure. Why?
Because he can always rest assured that
he succeeded in life's most important battle -
he defeated the fear of trying.

— Robert H. Schuller

*Keep your personal life and
your work life separate.*

Say "I love you" to those you love.
The eternal silence is long enough to be silent in,
and that awaits us all.

— George Eliot

*If you want to "get in touch with your feelings,"
fine - talk to yourself, we all do.
But if you want to communicate with another
thinking human being, get in touch with
your thoughts. Put them in order, give than
a purpose, use them to persuade, to instruct,
to discover, to seduce. The secret way to do
this is to write it down, and then cut out
the confusing parts.*

— William Safire

Straighten you problems out before you go to bed.
That way you will wake up smiling.

— Louis Fromm (married 55 years)

*Happiness is not the
absence of conflict but the ability to cope with it.*

The most important thing a father can do for his children is to love their mother.

*The grand essentials of happiness
are something to do, something to love,
and something to hope for.*

— Allan K. Chalmers

Beware of the danger signals that flag problems:
silence, secretiveness, or sudden outburst.

— Sylvia Porter

If you want to gather honey, don't kick the beehive.

— Dale Carnegie

*Thrice happy they whom an
unbroken bond unites,
And whom no quarrel shall sunder
before life's final day.*

— Horace

If you'd be loved, be worthy to be loved.

— Ovid

*A married man forms
married habits and becomes dependent of
marriage just as a sailor becomes
dependent of the sea.*

— George Bernard Shaw

Treasure each other in the recognition that we do not know how long we shall have each other.

— Joshua Loth Liebman

Grow old along with me!
The best is yet to be,
The last of life for which the
first was made.

— Robert Browning

If we spend our lives in loving, we have no leisure to complain, or to feel unhappiness.

— Joseph Joubert

In many ways do the full heart reveal
The presence of love it would conceal.

— Samuel Taylor Coleridge

The many make the household,
But only one the home.

— J. R. Lowell

*Happiness comes of the capacity to feel deeply,
to enjoy simply, to think freely, to be needed.*

— Storm Jameson

It is never too late to fall in love.

— Sandy Wilson

I love thee with breath,
Smiles, tears, of all my life.

— Elizabeth Barrett Browning

No matter whether you are on the road or in an argument, when you begin to see red, STOP!

*More homes are destroyed by fusses
than by funeral or fires.*

There is, indeed, nothing that so much seduces reason from vigilance, as the thought of passing life with an amiable woman.

Samuel Johnson